I love you
Grandpa

I love you Grandpa

Susan Akass

Illustrations by Hannah George

CICO BOOKS
LONDON NEW YORK

You'll play ball with me all afternoon.

You can mend ANYTHING.

Published in 2012 by CICO Books
An imprint of Ryland Peters & Small
519 Broadway, 5th Floor, New York NY 10012
20–21 Jockey's Fields, London WC1R 4BW
www.cicobooks.com

10 9 8 7 6 5 4 3 2 1

Text © Susan Akass 2012
Design and illustration © CICO Books 2012

A CIP catalog record for this book is available
from the Library of Congress and the British
Library.

ISBN: 978-1-908170-40-8

Printed in China

Design: David Fordham
Illustration: Hannah George

You are my grandpa, but I call you...

....

and I love you because...

When it snows, we go sledging together.

You whistle while you work.

You showed me
how to cook on a
camp fire.

You always fall asleep after dinner and I creep up and

tickle your ear!

You have **time to** play
L O N G
games of chess with me.

We had lots of FUN
raking up the leaves.

You took me
HIKING
and we walked for
MILES.

We visit museums,
and you tell me
fascinating facts.

We go fishing,
and once
We CAUGHT a

You pick me up
by my feet and
hold me
UPSIDE DOWN.

I helped you pick
strawberries.

You have to **put** SUN CREAM on your HEAD.

You Whistle
While you Work.

You make the
BEST sandwiches.

We try to touch
our NOSES with
our TONGUES.

We get up early and cook breakfast TOGETHER.

You CAN do incredible
magic tricks!

We polish your car until it SHINES.

You held my hand
when I tried out
my NEW skates.

You teach me how to read maps.

You make videos of me
doing SILLY things.

You're PROUD of all your homegrown vegetables.

I CAN work the TV better than YOU CAN.

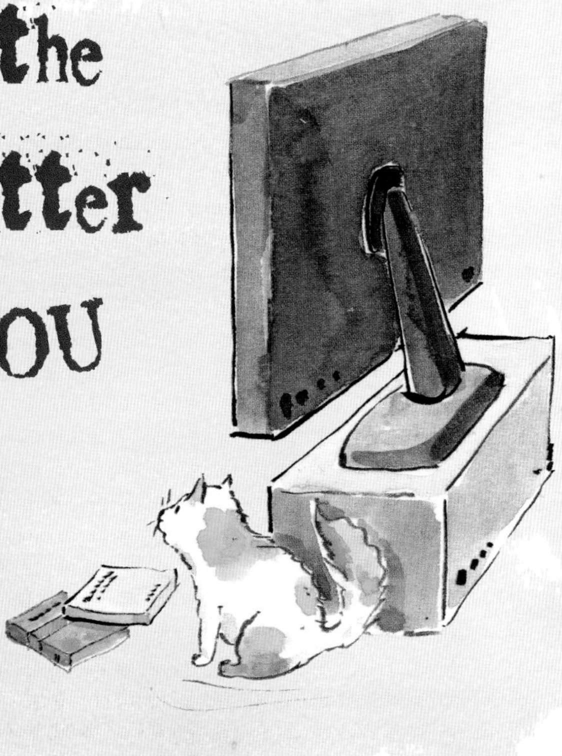

You bought a BIG

MOTORBIKE

and took me for a ride.

You bounce me
on your knee and
Sing silly songs.

You can make

AMAZING

stuff out of wood.

When you hear music, you pretend that you're the conductor.

You've got a BrisTLY mustache.

We sit in your shed
and have
MILK and **COOKIES.**

You taught me to play golf.

You oiled my bike
so now it
ZOOMS.

You NEVER let me beat

you at table tennis.

You can
mend ANYTHING.

When it snows, we go
sledging together.

You LAUGH at YOUR OWN JOKES.

We make MODEL BOATS together.

You push your glasses to the top of your head and forget where they are.

You'll play ball with me

ALL afternoon.

You're an inspiration!

I love you because...

1. ....

2. ....

3. ....

4. ....

5. ....